A Picture Book of Amelia Earhart

David A. Adler

illustrated by Jeff Fisher

For Cody,
David A. Adler

Holiday House/New York

For my niece, Ayelet Dora Adler
D. A. A.

To Noelle Brosch, who taught me how to work
J. F.

Library of Congress Cataloging-in-Publication Data
Adler, David A.
A picture book of Amelia Earhart / by David A. Adler; illustrated
by Jeff Fisher. — 1st ed.
p.   cm. — (A picture book biography)
Summary: Discusses the life of the pilot who was the first woman
to cross the Atlantic by herself in a plane.
ISBN 0-8234-1315-2 (reinforced)
1. Earhart, Amelia, 1897–1937—Juvenile literature.   2. Air
pilots—United States—Biography—Juvenile literature.
[1. Earhart, Amelia, 1897–1937.   2. Air pilots.   3. Women—
Biography.]   I. Fisher, Jeff, 1952–   . II. Title.   III. Series:
Adler, David A. Picture book biography.
TL540.E3A45   1998   96-54854   CIP   AC
629.13′092—dc21
[B]
ISBN 0-8234-1517-1 (pbk.)

Amelia Earhart was born in Atchison, Kansas, on July 24, 1897. Her parents were Edwin Earhart, a lawyer for a railroad, and Amy Earhart, the daughter of a wealthy judge. In 1900 the Earharts had a second daughter, Muriel.

Amelia was not a quiet schoolgirl. She threw mud balls, jumped over fences, played baseball and football, and shot her own .22 rifle to rid the family's barn of rats. When she was seven, she made her own roller coaster, using fence rails and a pair of old roller skates.

Although other girls their age wore long, ruffled dresses, Amelia and Muriel Earhart often wore loose fitting pants called bloomers. The Earhart girls' behavior was shocking to some people. But, Amelia wrote later, "Some elders have to be shocked for everybody's good now and then."

Amelia was eleven years old when she first saw an airplane. It was 1908, five years after the Wright brothers made the first successful flight. Amelia wrote later that at the time she thought it was just "a thing of rusty wire and wood . . . not at all interesting."

After high school, Amelia went to the Ogontz School in Pennsylvania. Amelia was tall and thin. In a letter to her parents from school she drew a sketch of herself dressed in a suit with a pleated skirt and wrote, "I look like a broom-stick wrapped round and round." And she wrote, "Did I tell you I have a reputation for brains?"

Amelia spent Christmas 1917 with her sister in Toronto, Canada. There she saw soldiers who had returned from the First World War. Years later, she wrote, "For the first time, I realized what the World War meant. Instead of new uniforms and brass bands, I saw only the results of four years' desperate struggle; men without arms and legs, men who were paralyzed, and men who were blind."

Soon after the holiday, Amelia quit school. She went back to Toronto, became a nurse's aide, and cared for the war wounded.

While Amelia was in Toronto she went to a nearby air-field and had another look at airplanes. Some years later she explained that "though I had seen one or two at county fairs before, I now saw many of them . . . I hung around in my spare time and absorbed all I could."

After the war Amelia studied automobile-engine repair. The next year she took courses in New York City, at Columbia University and Barnard College. At first she was preparing to study medicine. Later she decided to do medical research.

After the school year ended, Amelia went to be with her parents, who had moved to California. On Christmas Day 1920, she went to an airshow and three days later she paid one dollar for a ten-minute airplane ride. "As soon as I left the ground," she wrote later, "I knew I myself had to fly."

In January 1921, Amelia took her first flying lesson. In July she bought her first airplane. She paid for the lessons and airplane with money she earned working for the Los Angeles telephone company and with money given and loaned to her by her mother and sister.

Flying wasn't as safe then as it is today. Airplanes were powered by small engines. Amelia had several crash landings. Once she was thrown into an open field. Another time, her airplane turned over in heavy rain and Amelia, held in by her safety belt, hung upside down.

In 1924 Amelia's parents divorced. She sold her airplane and bought a yellow sports car and drove her mother east, to their new home in Medford, Massachusetts.

Sam Chapman, a chemical engineer, followed Amelia east. Chapman wanted Amelia to marry him, but Amelia refused to become what she called a "domestic robot." At the time she said, "I don't want to marry anyone."

On weekdays Amelia had a job as a social worker in a community center in nearby Boston, teaching English to immigrant children. On weekends she flew for "sport" and as a saleswoman for an airplane builder.

In May 1927 Charles Lindbergh became the first to fly across the Atlantic Ocean. The next year Amelia Earhart became the first woman to make the flight. She was co-passenger aboard an airplane named *Friendship*. In June 1928 Amelia, Bill Stultz, and Slim Gordon climbed into the *Friendship*. It was painted orange, so it would be easy to find in case of an accident and was fitted with pontoons, so if they couldn't complete the trip, they could land on the ocean. Before the trip Amelia telegraphed her mother, "Don't worry. No matter what happens, it will have been worth the trying."

While Stultz flew the plane, Amelia checked maps and kept a record of their speed and altitude. She also looked out the window at clouds she described as "marvelous shapes in white." She was, she wrote, "gulping beauty."

On June 18, 1928, after twenty hours and forty minutes in the air, the plane landed in the water, in the harbor of Burry Port, Wales. Amelia described the flight as "a grand experience," but since she didn't pilot the plane, she said she felt like "baggage."

When the three flyers returned to New York, they were given keys to the city. They were driven in open cars in a parade down Broadway. People leaned out office windows for a look and threw down confetti to celebrate.

Amelia Earhart was the first woman to fly across the Atlantic Ocean. She was an American heroine.

Amelia Earhart wrote a book and newspaper and magazine articles. She gave lectures and allowed her name to be used on luggage, clothing, stationery, and in advertisements. In her speeches she spoke against war and for the rights of women. Her schedule and endorsements were managed by her book publisher, George Putnam.

On February 7, 1931, Putnam became more than her publisher. He became her husband. Early the next year, at breakfast, Amelia told him she wanted to fly across the Atlantic Ocean again. This time she would pilot the airplane. She would go alone.

Amelia Earhart took off in a red and gold single engine airplane from Harbour Grace, Newfoundland, on May 20, 1932. She flew through strong winds, heavy rain, and thick clouds, often with the wings and windshield of her airplane covered with slush and ice, until she landed the next afternoon in a pasture in Londonderry, Northern Ireland. She said later that her landing "frightened all the cows in the neighborhood."

"Have you come far?" the first person to see her asked.

"From America," Amelia Earhart told him.

"Have you now?" the man said, not sure he could believe her.

With this flight Amelia Earhart became the very first woman, and just the second person after Charles Lindbergh to fly alone across the Atlantic Ocean. She became one of the most celebrated people of her time.

In June, President Herbert Hoover presented her with a gold medal, one of many awards she received for her great achievement. He called her a "pioneering" woman. Amelia Earhart said she just hoped her flight "has meant something to women in aviation."

It did. Amelia Earhart's many daring adventures meant a lot to women in all fields.

Amelia Earhart had other flying adventures. In January 1935 she became the first to fly from Hawaii to California. With that flight she also became the first to fly alone across both the Atlantic and Pacific oceans. In April she became the first to fly alone from Los Angeles to Mexico City.

In 1937 she planned to fly around the world. When she was told the flight was dangerous, Amelia said, "I've wanted to do this flight for a long time . . . If I should pop off, it will be doing the thing I've always wanted to do."

On June 1, 1937, Amelia Earhart and her navigator, Fred Noonan, began the trip. They flew from Miami, Florida, to San Juan, Puerto Rico. They flew to South America, then to Africa, India, Burma, Thailand, Singapore, Indonesia, Australia, and New Guinea. They had gone more than three fourths around the world. On July 2 they took off from Lae, New Guinea, for Howland Island, a tiny island in the vast Pacific Ocean.

They never made it.

Amelia Earhart and Fred Noonan disappeared somewhere in the Pacific Ocean. There was an enormous search, but they were never found.

Before she was lost, Amelia wrote to her husband, "I am quite aware of the hazards . . . I want to do it. Women must try to do things as men have tried. When they fail, their failures must be but a challenge to others."

Amelia Earhart was America's "First Lady of the Air." She was a courageous flyer, a pioneer. She risked her life to prove that in the air, and elsewhere, women were up to the challenge. She certainly was.

IMPORTANT DATES

1897   Born in Atchison, Kansas, on July 24.

1921   Had her first flying lesson on January 3 and bought her first airplane, the *Canary*, for her birthday.

1928   Flew aboard the *Friendship* and became the first woman to cross the Atlantic Ocean by air, June 17–18.

1931   Married George P. Putnam on February 7.

1932   Flew alone across the Atlantic, the first woman and just the second person to do it, May 20–21.

1935   Became the first person to fly from Hawaii to California, January 11–12.

1935   Became the first person to fly alone from Los Angeles to Mexico City, April 19–20.

1937   Disappeared in the Pacific Ocean, July 3.

AUTHOR'S NOTE

In 1890 Amelia's mother became the first woman to climb to the top of 14,110-foot high Pike's Peak in Colorado.

Amelia Earhart knew the flight from New Guinea to Howland Island was perhaps the most difficult part of her journey around the world. The island is just two miles long and less than a mile wide, a tiny bit of land in the great Pacific Ocean.

There have been many theories about Amelia Earhart's disappearance, including that she was on a secret mission for the United States government to spy on Pacific islands held by the Japanese who captured and killed her and Noonan. According to another theory she was held a prisoner of the Japanese until after the Second World War when she was brought back in secret to the United States. There is little evidence that there is any truth to these theories.

SELECTED BIBLIOGRAPHY

Backus, Jean L. *Letters From Amelia, 1901–1937*. Boston: Beacon Press, 1982.

Burke, John. *Winged Legend*. New York: G.P. Putnam's Sons, 1970.

Lovell, Mary S. *The Sound of Wings: The Life of Amelia Earhart*. New York: St. Martins Press, 1989.

New York Times. July 1937.

Putnam, George Palmer. *Soaring Wings: A Biography of Amelia Earhart*. New York: Harcourt, Brace and Company, 1939.

Rich, Doris L. *Amelia Earhart*. Washington, D.C.: Smithsonian Institution Press, 1989.

Other books in David A. Adler's *Picture Book Biography* series